# SUMMARY
# &ANALYSIS
## OF
# Atomic
# Habits

An Easy & Proven Way to
Build Good Habits & Break Bad Ones

A GUIDE TO THE BOOK
BY JAMES CLEAR

NOTE: This book is a summary and analysis and is meant as a companion to, not a replacement for, the original book.

Please follow this link to purchase a copy of the original book: https://amzn.to/2KWimPs

# TABLE OF CONTENTS

# SYNOPSIS

In high school, James Clear suffered a devastating brain injury after being hit in the head with an errant baseball bat. In the years that followed, he found himself forced to overcome multiple physical and mental ailments in order to be successful. When he got to college, he devoted himself to starting tiny habits—little things that would help him succeed—like keeping his room tidy or always getting enough sleep. From those habits, Clear was able to grow leaps and bounds to find significant academic and athletic success. After college, he started a blog writing about his personal experiments with habits. Over time, that website became so hugely popular, he was suddenly considered an expert on habits. Which brings us to this book.

*Atomic Habits* is a guide to creating small habits that will, over time, lead to massive change. Eating a little healthier or saving a little more money make not make much of a difference this month or even this year, but down the line, it adds up to monumental gains. But even knowing this, many people still can't stick to habits they know will be better later. Clear offers a step-by-step guide to change the way your brain responds to the habits you want and the ones you don't.

The book is broken down into six sections, the first of which focuses on the fundamentals of atomic habits and the theory behind them. The next four sections are devoted to the four laws of making and keeping a new habit: make it obvious, make it attractive, make it easy, and make it satisfying. Conversely, if you are trying to break a bad habit, you should do the opposite: make it invisible, make it unattractive, make it difficult, and make it unsatisfying. Each section provides real-world examples and specific advice. Lastly, Clear addresses some more advanced issues you may come across as you continue to develop and improve in your new habit, whatever that may be.

# PART I: THE FUNDAMENTALS

In 2003, the British cycling team was one of the worst in the world. From 2010-2017, that same team won 178 world championships and 66 Olympic or Paralympic gold medals. How did they make such a massive turnaround? The author presents evidence they used a combination of tiny, 1 percent improvements to accumulate into massive success.

## Key Takeaway: Both good and bad habits compound over time.

*"Habits are the compound interest of self-improvement"* (Clear, p. 15).

If you get 1 percent better every day, you'll be 37 times better in a year. If you get 1 percent worse every day, you'll basically become "zero." Clear gives numerous examples of how our tiny habits compound over time. Eating unhealthy today won't change the scale, but if we do it everyday, it will. If you're a millionaire now, but you're spending more than you earn, eventually you'll be broke. Conversely, if you're poor now but saving a little bit every day, eventually you'll have a lot more money. Every tiny habit in the right direction makes a noticeable difference over time. That's why cultivating the good ones is so important.

## Key Takeaway: Compounding habits have breakthrough moments.

Clear notes that it is tempting to abandon good habits when results aren't seen in a few weeks or months, but that many habits have a breakthrough point where things will suddenly become visible to you. He terms this frustrating first stage as "the plateau of latent potential" (p. 21). Like an ice cube slowly warming to thirty-two degrees without melting or an earthquake happening after millions of years of tectonic stress, many big changes aren't noticeable at all until they break through.

## Key Takeaway: Focus on systems over goals to achieve success.

If setting a goal was enough to achieve it, then every single Olympian would win a gold medal. The difference between success and failure isn't setting goals, but focusing on the *process*. What systems dictate how you operate? What are you doing to achieve that goal? How often do you practice? How do you study for a test? If you have the right system in place, then the goals should come naturally. "Fix the inputs and the outputs will fix themselves" (Clear, p. 25).

Additionally, when you're focused on achieving goals, you can often end up pinning your happiness to that success. Once that goal is complete, what happens next? Or what if you don't achieve it? Focusing on systems means you can be happy so long as your system is running smoothly, no matter what that looks like for you.

Lastly, focusing on goals can mean losing motivation once you achieve that goal. If you're focused on your process, there are always tweaks to be made and room to improve.

## Key Takeaway: There are three layers of behavior change: outcomes, processes, and identity.

When most people want to change something, they focus on the outcome: I want to be skinnier. The next thing people look towards is the process: I will eat healthier foods. But what Clear argues is that neither of these things get to the core of the problem with the habit. Anyone can eat healthier for a couple of weeks, but if that's not who you identify yourself as, you will fall back into your old habits. Rather than saying "I'm trying to eat heathier" you should say "I'm a healthy eater." It's a small difference he argues, but one that changes the way we view the decisions we make. The goal is not to lose weight, but to *become* a healthy eater.

## Key Takeaway: Your actions follow your identity.

If you identify as a smoker, trying to quit will be just that: trying. If you identify as a non-smoker, then having a cigarette doesn't fit within your idea of yourself. Clear argues that in order to make lasting change, we have to change our own identity. Oftentimes, we are unable to change because our self-perception tells us it isn't who we are. Thoughts like

"I'm not a morning person" or "I'm no good with technology" reinforce ideas that we can't do something.

In order to change your identity, you have to slowly build the habits of the person you want to become. Writing for one hour doesn't make you a writer, but if you write a little bit, every day, then you begin to embody the identity of a writer, and soon you'll begin to see yourself as one. If you want to lose weight, ask yourself what kind of things a healthy person would do. Would they take the stairs or the elevator? Have a salad or a pizza?

Clear recommends two steps:

1.   Decide the type of person you want to be.

2.   Prove it to yourself with small wins. (p. 39)

Small actions and habits matter because eventually they can change your own beliefs about yourself.

## Key Takeaway: A habit is an automatic behavior for your brain.

Our brains are endlessly trying to be as efficient as possible. When we are able to make a habit of something, our brains are able to do it automatically without using conscious brain power. Since your brain wants to conserve as much power as possible, it actively seeks out habits to streamline its response time. A habit, for your brain, allows it to solve a problem in as little time with as little energy as possible. Maybe when you move into your new house, you're always forgetting the light switch is on the other side of the room. But then you learn, and you never have to think about it again. The brain performs these efficiency tests constantly.

## Key Takeaway: The habit loop involves four steps: cue, craving, response, and reward.

Every habit is created and reinforced using these four steps, whether it is a good habit or a bad one. Here is an example: you get a stressful email from your boss (cue), which makes you want to relax or escape for a minute (craving), so you go grab a doughnut from the conference room (response). Your problem is solved, you have achieved relaxation (reward). The next time you get a stressful email from your boss, you may go through the exact same cycle. The cycle is an endless feedback loop; the more you do it, the more it reinforces itself. This is why old habits are so hard to break. Eventually, you don't even realize the email is what made you crave a doughnut.

## Key Takeaway: You can break habits using the Four Laws of Behavior Change.

In order to create a good habit you should try to structure the four stages of the feedback loop to follow these rules (p. 54):

**Cue** – Make it obvious

**Craving** – Make it attractive

**Response** – Make it easy

**Reward** – Make it satisfying

Conversely, to break a bad habit, you would want an invisible cue, an unattractive craving, a response that is difficult to do, and a reward that isn't very satisfying.

The following chapters will address exactly how to implement these four rules in your daily life.

# PART II: MAKE IT OBVIOUS

Key Takeaway: Move your habits from unconscious to conscious.

The problem with our habits is that, for the most part, we're completely unaware of them. The more we perform a particular behavior, the more ingrained it becomes, and the less we think about it. In order to force our habits to become more visible, Clear recommends two techniques: pointing-and-calling and making a Habits Scorecard.

Pointing-and-calling is a method utilized by Japanese train conductors to reduce accidents on the track. Each of the engineers points to each element of the train before arriving or departing from the station. For example, one would say "The light is green" while pointing to the light. Though this may seem silly, the act of making the mental checklist a physical and audible process shifts it from unconscious to conscious. In your own life, you may use pointing-and-calling before you leave the house to make sure you haven't forgotten anything.

A Habits Scorecard can be helpful in rooting out behaviors that are second nature to you. From the moment you wake up, track every single action you take during the day. Such as, "wake up, hit snooze button, wake up for real, turn off alarm, brush teeth, etc." Then review all of the habits and decide if they are positive, negative, or neutral. You want to think in the long term: does this action help me become the person I want to be? If not, then it's a negative habit that you'll want to work on changing. For example, if you didn't hit the snooze button, you could use those ten extra minutes in the morning to read the paper or do a few stretches.

## Key Takeaway: Implementation intention increases your chances of success.

Implementation intention means specifically defining what you intend to do and when. Rather than say "I'm going to work out this week," say, "I'm going to run for thirty minutes on Wednesday at 7 a.m." You can do this more generally with habits, saying "Whenever X happens, I will do Y in response." Defining these actions means taking the guess work out of the next step. Many people fail because their goals are too broad; in order to move forward, they have to make an additional decision about when, where, and how. Instead, make rules for yourself such as "If there are stairs, I will take them instead of the elevator."

## Key Takeaway: Habit Stacking increases the likelihood of building a new habit.

Our lives are full of cues from one behavior to the next: every time we go to the bathroom, then we wash our hands, which reminds us to put the towels in the laundry. Clear argues that you can use existing habits in order to strengthen new habits by "stacking" them. If you have a cup of coffee every morning, then read the news, you could stack a habit right after it such as meditating or writing in your journal. After you meditate, your next habit could be to put the dishes away. Always one after the other. You can stack habits on top of existing habits or even squeeze them in between steps of your normal routine. The key is to be very specific about when and how your new habit will fit in. "I will read more at night" is far more vague than "After I brush my teeth, I will read for 20 minutes." Always be as specific as possible.

## Key Takeaway: Your environment dictates your behavior.

In a study done at a hospital cafeteria, making the water bottles more prominently displayed than the soda decreased soda consumption and increased water consumption significantly—changing your environment can change your behavior.

If you want to read more at night, keep a book on your pillow. If you want to eat more fruit, keep it in a bowl on the counter rather than hidden in the fridge. Additionally, Clear recommends a "one space, one purpose" rule. If you watch TV and browse social media in bed, it will be harder to get to sleep. If you frequently play video games on the couch, it will be harder to get work done in that room. Organize your life so that each space is dedicated to a single purpose. When you do this, the context of the space will trigger cues in your brain to perform the action associated with that space. For those who work from home especially, designating work vs. living spaces is crucial to maintaining work/life balance.

## Key Takeaway: To break bad habits, make them invisible.

The key to self-control is to structure your environment to avoid having to use it. Successful people aren't necessarily stronger or have more willpower than others, they simply create environments that mean they don't have to use as much self-control in the first place. Our environments are such strong cues for our behaviors that it is nearly impossible to break a bad habit if you don't change the environment in which the habit was first formed. You must reduce your exposure to the cue that causes the bad habit. If you're watching too much TV at night, take the TV out of your bedroom. If you're eating too many cookies, stop buying cookies or put them in a hard-to-reach place. Once a habit is formed, it is almost impossible to erase the pathways in the brain—you must instead remove the cues that lead to the behavior.

# PART III: MAKE IT ATTRACTIVE

### Key Takeaway: Habits are a dopamine-driven feedback loop.

Most people are aware that dopamine is part of the reward system in the brain. Dopamine levels affect our desires, motivations, learning, punishment, aversion, and voluntary movement (Clear, p. 106). When someone likes your status on Facebook, you get a hit of dopamine. When a cocaine addict *sees* the drug (before even ingesting it) they get an even bigger hit. The same is true *before* a gambler places a bet or when you *anticipate* any coming reward. The dopamine from anticipation causes us to take action to get another dopamine hit when we receive the reward. This cue is incredibly powerful.

### Key Takeaway: Use temptation bundling to make habits more attractive.

Temptation bundling is when you attach a habit you don't find particularly attractive (like working out) to one that you do find attractive (like watching Netflix)—one is something you *want* to do, the other is something you *need* to do. In an example provided by the author, an engineering student rigged his television to only play if he maintained a certain speed on a stationary bicycle. Similarly, you could get a pedicure, but only if you spend the time catching up on work emails, or listen to a podcast you love, but only while cleaning the kitchen.

You can also attach your temptation bundling to the habit stacking you learned in the last section. The formula is:

After [CURRENT HABIT], I will [HABIT I NEED]. After [HABIT I NEED], I will [HABIT I WANT].

(Clear, p. 110)

If social media is a reward for you, then tell yourself "After I finish my morning meeting, I will do 20 sit-ups. After I do 20 sit-ups, I will check Facebook." You may even get excited to do the sit-ups because your brain will *anticipate* the reward of checking Facebook when you start the less desirable behavior.

## Key Takeaway: Culture and society determine which behaviors are attractive.

Belonging is a natural part of human survival and we will always be motivated to imitate and fit in with those around us. Whether the culture around us reinforces good habits or bad ones, we will naturally, unconsciously be inclined to imitate those habits. Clear advises that the only way to succeed in changing an ingrained behavior is to join a culture where that behavior is the norm. Want to start running every day? Make friends with other people who do the same.

Becoming part of a group solidifies behavior as part of your identity, which we have learned is crucial to long-term change. If changing your habits means going against the tribe, it will be that much harder for you to accomplish it. The change might ostracize you, which is a very unattractive prospect for humans.

## Key Takeaway: Your cravings are based on deep, evolutionary needs.

You may think you want a taco because they're delicious or you want to play video games because they're fun. But the reality is you want a taco because of a deep-seated evolutionary need for survival. The video games may offer you a sense of belonging with your online friends or may help you win social approval. All of our actions can be traced back to fulfilling basic human needs for survival. Any habits that fulfill these needs are innately attractive to us as humans, so we must reframe the hard habits to also fulfill our basic needs. If you want to start running, joining that running group can mean exercise is fulfilling your evolutionary need for belonging.

## Key Takeaway: Change the way you talk about hard habits to make them more enjoyable.

Clear recommends a simple word change: rather than saying you *have* to do something, say you *get* to do something. "I have to go running this morning" sends a different cue to our brains than saying "I get to go running this morning" or "I get to improve my endurance."

Clear gives examples of several other habits that are hard to start such as meditation, saving money, and exercise. You can reframe any of these habits in your brain as positives rather than negatives. You can also use a motivation ritual to help trigger a difficult habit. If you always play the same music before you exercise, hearing that song will eventually trigger your brain to prepare for a workout.

# PART IV: MAKE IT EASY

## Key Takeaway: Focus on action instead of motion.

It is easy to get caught up in planning the best way to lose weight or opining on twenty different articles you could write. Instead, just get started. Don't research diets online, start by making a healthy meal. Today. Motion allows you to feel like you're making progress without actually doing anything. Preparation is its own form of procrastination. Practice and repetition are the only ways to form a habit. The more you *do* it, the better you get. Planning and preparation don't build habits.

## Key Takeaway: The brain rewires itself with increased repetition.

The more you perform a particular action, the stronger the connection between those neurons grows, and the more instinctive the behavior becomes. This end result of this is known as automaticity: when you can perform a behavior without even thinking about it. Clear provides evidence that automaticity is determined by the number of repetitions, not by the amount of time spent on the activity. There is no rule for a habit to be formed in thirty days or twenty or sixty—the more frequently you perform it, the sooner it will become a habit.

## Key Takeaway: Our brains naturally gravitate towards the easiest solution.

Being lazy is beneficial to our brains and bodies—it conserves energy. Doing 100 push-ups a day is hard. Much harder than watching TV. The trick is to make your habits easier. One example of this is joining a gym on your existing route to work. The less friction your new habit introduces, the more likely you will be to stick to it. Clear recommends "priming your environment" as much as possible to make your habit as easy as possible.

If you want to exercise in the morning, set out your workout clothes the night before. If you want to eat healthier, chop the veggies at the beginning of the week. This works conversely for bad behaviors as well. Make it harder for yourself to watch TV by unplugging it, or leave your phone in another room to avoid checking it.

## Key Takeaway: Use the Two-Minute Rule to form gateway habits.

Running a 10K or writing a novel might seem like nearly impossible tasks to conquer. But Clear recommends, in order to form any new habit, take a two-minute chunk and start there. Read one page of a book every night; write for two minutes in your journal; put on your workout clothes every day (but don't start working out). Eventually, the beginning of the habit will be enough to put your brain into the right mindset to go further along. It will feel silly not to.

Also remember that many habits occur at "decisive moments" that can send the rest of your day on a productive or unproductive path. Skipping the morning workout can make you feel lazy and lead to having a less healthy lunch. Start creating small cues to help you take the better fork in the road each time.

## Key Takeaway: Use a commitment device to make bad habits difficult or impossible.

A commitment device forces you to forgo a bad habit by physically removing it from possibility. If you don't want to spend money on lunch, don't bring your wallet along; if you don't want to use social media, install a program that will block specific sites on a timer. Turn off chat notifications or delete games and apps on your phone. Change your environment so it takes more work to engage in the bad habit than the good one. The author had his assistant reset his social media passwords every Monday so he was locked out until Friday.

## Key Takeaway: Use technology in your favor.

One of the greatest things about technology is how much easier it makes it to create good habits. There are apps that will automatically save money for you and meal programs that will deliver healthy meal kits to your door. While technology is also dangerous (who hasn't been on a Netflix binge?) there are countless ways it can make your good habits that much easier to stick to. Whatever habit you're trying to start or stop, do a little research and see if there's an app for that—there probably already is.

# PART IV: MAKE IT SATISFYING

Key Takeaway: We are more likely to repeat a behavior when the experience is *immediately* satisfying.

Humans evolved to live in an "immediate-return environment" where the payoff to our actions is quick. If we eat, we aren't hungry; if we find shelter, we get warmer. But our environment today is a delayed-return environment. If you exercise today, you won't lose weight today. If you save a little money each paycheck, it will take years to build up enough to retire. Unfortunately, most bad habits tend to have immediate rewards but long-term negatives, whereas most good habits are less enjoyable in the now but more beneficial over time.

## Key Takeaway: Attach immediate reinforcement to your good habits.

The trick to overcoming a delayed-return environment is to attach immediately satisfying actions to your habits in order to entice your brain to do them again and again. While the previous three rules focus on getting you to perform a habit the first time, the fourth rule focuses on getting you to do it again—it completes the habit-feedback loop. If you want to drink less alcohol, you experience no immediate reward for sitting at home with a glass of water. Clear recommends creating a gratification system. For example, every time you skip a happy hour, you could transfer $20 into a savings account towards taking a trip or buying a special item. Note that your reward for the behavior should not conflict with the identity you want: the reward for exercising should NOT be a bowl of ice cream; the reward for saving more money should not be buying a big-ticket item.

## Key Takeaway: Use visual markers or habit trackers to denote progress.

When working towards a large goal such as writing a book, it can often be difficult to see your own progress. Clear recommends "The Paper Clip Strategy" where each time you make a small bit of progress, you move a paper clip from one jar to another. Visual progress reinforces the good behavior and strengthens the habit. Another excellent method is a habit tracker. You can mark off days on a calendar you have performed your habit. One of the cardinal rules this enforces is "don't break the chain." No matter what, perform your habit every day (or however often you are meant to perform it).

Seeing the streak of success in your habit tracker will motivate you to keep going and keep you honest with yourself. It is also satisfying—seeing progress is an immediate reward tied to your good behavior.

## Key Takeaway: Perfection is not possible.

No matter how good you are at tracking and sticking to your habits, life will always manage to get in the way at some point. Clear's solution to this is to "never miss twice." As soon as one streak ends, jump right back into the next one. It's fine you ate pizza for lunch, but then be sure to have a salad for dinner. Too many people lose hope when they slip up and end up giving up entirely.

*"When successful people fail, they rebound quickly"* (Clear, p. 201)

If you're having a hard day and don't feel like working out, then just work out a little. Showing up is more than half the battle.

## Key Takeaway: Add immediate pain to deter negative habits with a habit contract or accountability partner.

In general, the more immediate and tangible the consequence for a behavior is, the more likely it is to influence your behavior. Vague and delayed consequences don't have as much as an impact. In order to implement these consequences, form a habit contract with one or two friends. The contract will stipulate exactly the consequences if you break the habits you're trying to create. Maybe you have to give your wife $100 if you skip the gym one day. Whatever it is, the repercussions must be immediate and painful. An accountability partner is simply a friend with whom you agree to perform the same habit. If you both don't do it, you are accountable to one another. Letting someone else down or breaking a contract with a friend is a far more painful motivator than breaking a contract with yourself.

# PART V: ADVANCED TACTICS

Key Takeaway: There are five main genetic traits that contribute to your personality.

Those traits are openness to experience, conscientiousness, extroversion, agreeableness, and neuroticism. Depending on your genetic makeup, some habits may be easier or harder for you to adopt. Clear recommends that in order to be successful, you try to identify areas in which you are more genetically prone to succeed. A person who is high in agreeableness may be naturally more inclined to start writing thank-you cards, for example. A less orderly person will have a harder time with a habit tracker and may require more environmental cues to stay on track. Use your personality traits to build habits and systems that work better for you, whether that means a low-fat diet over a low-carb one or reading steamy romance novels over Russian classics.

Key Takeaway: Explore/exploit to find the right habits.

Pick a habit that will be easier for you and you are more likely to be successful. Maybe you don't like running—try rock climbing, rowing, or playing tennis. If you start getting good at one, stick with it. Clear refers to this as "explore/exploit." Exploit if you're winning, and go back to exploring if it's not a good fit. Ask yourself if you're getting better returns than the average person. Have you ever felt "in the zone?" What were you doing?

## Key Takeaway: If you're not good at the game, make one up.

Clear acknowledges that most people will never become an Olympic swimmer or a bestselling author. But he believes that everyone can be the best at a specific thing—everyone has a unique combination of talents that can be exploited to create an entirely new field. The creator of the cartoon Dilbert wasn't a great comedian or a great artist. But he was a comedian with a business background who could draw, which gave him a unique advantage. Specialization is the key to success. Clear recommends you work hard at the things that come easy to you in order to find the most success. It may take some trial and error to find out what your niche is, but it will be far easier than struggling towards an activity or identity that doesn't come naturally to you.

## Key Takeaway: Work on tasks of "just manageable difficulty."

Any task you're working on should be just at the edge of your current ability, slightly beyond it. You wouldn't want to play tennis against a four-year-old, or against Serena Williams; one is easy and boring, the other leads to inevitable failure. According to studies, functioning in this "Goldilocks zone" provides optimal motivation and improvement.

## Key Takeaway: Boredom is normal.

Many people may believe that successful people have endless amounts of passion for their craft. The truth is that the successful people are the ones who keep showing up, day in and day out, despite the boredom that comes with doing the same thing over and over again. The more you do something, like publish a blog post or go to the gym, the more routine it becomes, and the less novel. Humans desire change and novelty. The Goldilocks rule will help mitigate this by keeping tasks just challenging enough, but it won't eliminate it. Clear suggests instead that you "fall in love with boredom." Professionals continue to do the work no matter what mood they're in or how they feel.

## Key Takeaway: Creating habits can lead to complacency.

The problem when we create an automatic habit is that it becomes so easy, we stop trying to improve. Clear suggests after each level of habit automation, you strive to reach the next level, until that level is internalized, and then you move to the next. A basketball player must be able to dribble without thinking before he can work on his three-pointer. The way to avoid slipping into this complacency is to create a system of reflection and review: you must be able to measure your current level of achievement in order to determine if you're getting better.

## Key Takeaway: Review and reflect to measure your progress, make adjustments, and stay on track.

The author creates an annual reflection on his progress each year: *How many articles did I write? How many new places did I visit? What went well? What could have gone better?*

He also makes an Integrity Report to assess if he is living in alignment with his own identity and core values. This is especially helpful as you are beginning to build up a new piece of your identity such as becoming a person who works out or becoming a writer. Clear warns the reader, however, not to tie their identity too much to one thing. If your whole identity is "I am a CEO" and then you lose your job, you may feel utterly lost. To mitigate this, instead tie your identity to the type of person you are (or want to be). Such as "I am a dedicated and reliable person who never gives up." This way you can be more flexible if you face a major life change. The rigid will fail; only those able and willing to adapt and change will be successful in life.

# EDITORIAL REVIEW

James Clear's *Atomic Habits* is a simple, straightforward guide to making big changes in your life through tiny, incremental improvements. If you keep improving by one percent, eventually you will be twice as good. If you keep getting worse by one percent, eventually you'll have nothing. These concepts can be applied (and are in the book) to any habit or behavior one can think of, though the most commonly used examples are likely the ones most people are interested in learning. These include saving money, dieting, working out, being more active, and watching less TV, among others. Whatever the habit you're trying to create or break, *Atomic Habits* offers an actionable, easy-to-follow guide to success.

Each part opens with a story or anecdote of a person who has applied atomic habits to their own success. The book is rich with real-world examples to help illustrate the power of small changes. The writing in the book is easily accessible, and while most of the evidence is anecdotal rather than scientific, this doesn't detract from the advice overall. Building better habits welcomes relatable, motivational examples. The main structure of the book—the four rules to creating lasting habits—are also easy to follow, and Clear provides helpful guides and tools throughout. At the end of each chapter, the author recaps the main points and provides an updated "cheatsheet" to remind you what you have just learned about breaking bad habits and creating good ones. You can find this cheatsheet on his website at http://atomichabits.com/cheatsheet. Please note, you must sign up for his email list to access it.

While the concept of atomic habits is certainly novel compared to many other habit-forming how-to guides, the bulk of the book is nothing new. Clear reveals no new science behind habit-forming, and if you have read any books about creating negative and positive reward systems to reinforce your habits, you'll be familiar with most of what you're reading. The real benefit to Clear's book is instead in his relatable writing, his clear analogy, and his focusing on working towards becoming the person you want to be, rather than focusing on changing a specific habit. Somewhat ironically, the "tiny steps" of atomic habits are actually steps towards a much bigger change.

In the appendix, Clear provides a more detailed breakdown of the four laws and how you may see them in action in everyday life. For anyone who left the book feeling confused or unfulfilled, this may help bring it home a little more. Additionally, he provides specific advice to those looking to apply his system to business or parenting, though not in the book itself. These "chapters" can instead be found on his website at atomichabits.com/business and atomichabits.com/parenting, respectively.

Whether you've read every book out on there on making or breaking habits, or if this is your first foray into a new and better you, Clear's book is a worthwhile read. Most of all, it offers hope and motivation to those who struggle with getting started or giving up too quickly when gratification is delayed.

# BACKGROUND ON AUTHOR

James Clear is an American author, entrepreneur, and photographer. His work has been published in dozens of major news media outlets including the *New York Times*, *Entrepreneur*, *TIME*, and *Business Insider*, among others. Most of his work is focused on the topics of habits, decision making, and continuous improvement.

James is a regular speaker at Fortune 500 companies and his methods have been used by teams in the NFL, NBA, and MLB. He attended Denison University where he was selected as the top male athlete, named to the ESPN Academic All-America Team, and received the President's Medal, all after suffering a devastating head injury in high school.

*Atomic Habits* is his first book.

*If you enjoyed this ZIP Reads publication, we encourage you to purchase a copy of <u>the original book.</u>*

*We'd also love an honest review on Amazon.com!*

# ZIPREADS

Manufactured by Amazon.ca
Bolton, ON